Keto Copycat Recipes

Tasty and Accurate Ketogenic Recipes from the Most Popular Restaurants to Replicate at Home

Lara Brooke

work can be in any fashion deemed liable for any hardship or damages that may befall them after undertaking information described herein.

Additionally, the information in the following pages is intended only for informational purposes and should thus be thought of as universal. As befitting its nature, it is presented without assurance regarding its prolonged validity or interim quality. Trademarks that are mentioned are done without written consent and can in no way be considered an endorsement from the trademark holder.

TABLE OF CONTENTS

Introduction

Copycat Recipes recreate popular restaurant dishes at home. If you are on the Keto Diet, this can be a big issue as most restaurants offer very few keto-friendly choices. But there is a solution, make favorite restaurant recipes keto-friendly! So, this is the cookbook for you!

Get ready to find out trendy and fun recipes for all hours of the day. Cooking itself is a tremendous pleasure - practicing self-love, spending time and effort learning, and preparing delicious food for yourself, your family, and friends.

The Copycat Recipes also give you some secret tips on some of your favorite restaurants and show you how easy it is to make homemade versions and great food.

Going out to dinner with your family and friends is laughing and enjoying a fantastic meal, having nothing too easy after dinner. But while you see the bill in front of your desk and pay an expensive amount for a single serving of food, is it worth it?
That's just one of the many advantages you can have by replicating these recipes at home.

Another important aspect is that you will always be sure that you are using quality products.

Whether you need to prepare a dinner for the whole family or have fun with co-workers and best friends, with Keto Copycat, you are sure to serve an unforgettable meal to please your family and friends.

Recipes that simulate the same taste, including your favorite meal's flavor, but with a low carbohydrate content.

This cookbook is full of Keto Copycat Recipes from your favorite restaurants that you can make at home whenever you want.

Keto Copycat Recipes

Breakfast Souffle

Time required:
45 minutes

Servings: 04

INGREDIENTS

For Puff Pastry:
¼ cup almond flour
1 tablespoon coconut flour
5 tablespoons psyllium husks
¼ teaspoon baking powder
1 teaspoon xanthan gum
⅛ teaspoon salt
½ cup cold butter, chopped
1 egg white
½ cup cold water
For Souffle:
3 large eggs

STEPS FOR COOKING

1. For the pastry using a food processor, pulse the flours, psyllium husks, baking powder, xanthan gum, and salt into a fine powder.
2. Add the butter and pulse until coated.
3. Transfer the mixture to a bowl.
4. Add the egg white and cold water and mix with a spoon until a rough dough forms.
5. Knead to form a dough ball.
6. Cover the dough ball with plastic wrap and refrigerate for about 30 minutes.
7. Preheat the oven to 400°F.
8. For the soufflé, in a bowl, beat the eggs lightly.
9. Add the Parmesan cheese, sour cream, hot sauce, baking powder, garlic powder, and salt and mix well.

INGREDIENTS	STEPS FOR COOKING
¼ cup Parmesan cheese, finely grated	10. Add the spinach and bacon and stir to combine.
2 tablespoons sour cream	11. Place the dough between 2 lightly floured sheets of parchment paper and roll it out with a rolling pin.
1–2 dashes of hot sauce	12. Refrigerate until ready to use.
½ teaspoon baking powder	13. Cut the dough into four squares.
¼ teaspoon garlic powder	14. Place the pastry squares in the bottoms of four 4-inch tart pans and press slightly.
¼ teaspoon salt	15. Divide the spinach mixture among the pans and sprinkle with Asiago cheese.
¼ cup cooked bacon, chopped	16. Bake for 24–26 minutes or until the eggs are puffy.
¼ cup frozen chopped spinach, thawed	17. Serve warm.
¼ cup Asiago cheese, grated	

Cheese Toast

Time required:
15 minutes

Servings: 12

INGREDIENTS

12 slices pre-sliced soft white bread

1 cup unchilled butter

1.5 cups Parmesan cheese

Optional:

1 clove - minced garlic

Dried herbs: Rosemary - oregano or parsley

STEPS FOR COOKING

1. Whip the butter using a stand mixer or by hand until it's fluffy.

2. Shred and fold in the cheese - whip until combined (1-2 min.).

3. Spread a thick layer of the mixture over each bread slice.

4. Warm a large skillet on med-high-temperature.

5. Arrange the slices buttered side down and heat for one to two minutes until the butter and cheese spread is golden and the backside is softened.

6. Garnish as desired with the optional fixings.

Chick Fil a Sandwich

Time required:
30 minutes

Servings: 04

INGREDIENTS

For Marinade:

2 cups of water

2 cubes of chicken stock

1/4 teaspoon of seasoned salt

For Breadcrumbs:

1 cup of general-purpose flour

1 1/2 cup finely ground salty cracker crumbs

2 teaspoons of powdered sugar

1/4 teaspoon paprika

Ingredients for Sandwiches:

4 hamburger buns

STEPS FOR COOKING

Chicken Marinade Procedure:

1. Add blood-free water to the bowl, add 1/4 teaspoon of seasoned salt, and dissolve the mixture's stock cube. Place bird breasts in water, mix, cover, and refrigerate for 12 hours or the next day.

Chicken Dough Steps:

1. Drain and discard the chicken marinade. It cannot be reused. In a small bowl, combine all-purpose flour, crackers, powdered sugar, and paprika. Shuffle to combine.

2. Shake off the extra marinade and sprinkle some flour over the bird.

3. Place the beaten breasts on a rope rack and let them sit for a few minutes.

Cooking Chicken:

INGREDIENTS

8 pickles with dill

2 tablespoons of butter

You can use vegetable oil with peanut oil for frying

STEPS FOR COOKING

1. Heat the oil up to 350 steps in a tempura pan or large pan. If you are using a large pot, upload enough oil to be 4 inches deep.

2. Cook the poultry for 7-8 minutes or until the meat turns brown and the internal temperature reaches 165 ° C. Drain the bird in a clean cord rack.

3. Melt the butter and smooth with a burger roll.

4. Place a poultry sandwich on each bottom of the burger—pickles of two dill and top bread.

Hash Brown Casserole

Time required:
75 minutes

Servings: 08

INGREDIENTS

2 cup shredded
cheddar and
Monterey jack
cheese, divided

3 cups cauliflower
florets, cut small

1 tablespoon onion,
minced

1 cup sour cream

½ cup mayonnaise

¼ cup butter
softened

1 tablespoon
bouillon powder

1 teaspoon salt

½ teaspoon pepper

STEPS FOR COOKING

1. Preheat the oven to 350°F.
2. Grease an 8×8-inch baking dish.
3. In a bowl, stir together 1 cup of cheese and the remaining ingredients.
4. Place the mixture in the prepared baking dish and sprinkle it with the remaining cheese.
5. Bake for 50–60 minutes until the top is golden and bubbly.
6. Serve hot.

Bacon Temptation Omelet

Time required:
13 minutes

Servings: 01

INGREDIENTS

4 eggs

6 slices bacon, divided

.25 cups shredded Monterey Jack Cheese

4 oz. American cheese

2 tbsp. milk - Unsweetened almond, divided for use

2 tbsp. optional: Pancake batter

STEPS FOR COOKING

1. Warm a skillet or griddle to 350° Fahrenheit/177° Celsius.

2. Cook the bacon and set it aside. When it's cooled a bit, break it apart.

3. Arrange the American cheese in a saucepan.

4. Add milk (1 tbsp.) into the pan and heat the saucepan using the medium temperature setting.

5. Stir the cheese and milk continuously with a wooden spoon till the cheese melts.

6. Use the low-temperature setting to thicken the cheese sauce. Adjust the setting to low and stir until the cheese sauce thickens.

7. Break eggs into a mixing container. Add bacon bits (4 slices cooked), the remaining tablespoon of milk, and

INGREDIENTS	STEPS FOR COOKING

pancake batter. Whisk until everything blends smoothly.

8. Lightly spritz a skillet or griddle or skillet using a bit of cooking oil spray. Pour the mixture of eggs, bacon, pancake batter, and milk onto the griddle in a rectangular shape. As the mixture is cooked, the omelet is formed.

9. When the omelet is almost prepared, pour ½ of the cheese sauce over the omelet and roll it. Sprinkle cheese and remaining small pieces of bacon on the top of the omelet.

10. Your bacon temptation omelet is ready to serve. Serve it with the remaining cheese sauce on its side if desired.

Keto French Toast

Time required:
10 minutes

Servings: 03

INGREDIENTS

8 slices of Texas toast or sourdough bread

4 eggs

1 cup of milk

2 tablespoons of sugar

4 teaspoons vanilla extract

2 pinches of salt

Butter and syrup for serving

STEPS FOR COOKING

1. Beat the eggs, milk, sugar, vanilla, and salt together in a large bowl.

2. Heat a griddle or skillet over medium heat. Spray with nonstick cooking spray.

3. Dip each sandwich in the egg mixture and let it soak for 25-30 seconds on all sides.

4. Place the slices on the baking sheet or skillet and cook for 2-3 minutes on all sides or until golden brown.

5. Serve with butter and syrup.

Lemon Poppy Seed Bread

Time required:
45 minutes

Servings: 14

INGREDIENTS

2 cups almond flour

⅓ cup erythritol

1 teaspoon poppy seeds

1 teaspoon baking powder

2 eggs

¼ cup butter, melted

¼ cup sour cream

2 tablespoons lemon juice

1 teaspoon lemon extract

1 teaspoon lemon zest

STEPS FOR COOKING

1. Preheat the oven to 350°F.
2. Line a loaf pan with parchment paper.
3. In a bowl, mix together the flour, erythritol, poppy seeds, and baking powder.
4. Add the remaining ingredients and mix well.
5. Place the dough in the prepared loaf pan, then bake for about 30 minutes or until a toothpick inserted in the center comes out clean.
6. Remove the loaf pan from the oven and place it on a wire rack for about 10 minutes.
7. Carefully invert the bread loaf onto the wire rack to cool completely before serving.
8. Slice and serve.

Cheddar Biscuits

Time required:
20 minutes

Servings: 10

INGREDIENTS

4 eggs

1 cup almond flour

2 tsp. baking powder

Black pepper (as desired)

2 cups cheddar cheese, shredded

1 tsp garlic powder

2 tbsp. melted butter

1 tbsp. fresh parsley

STEPS FOR COOKING

1. Set the oven temperature at 400° Fahrenheit/204° Celsius.

2. Prepare a baking tray using a silicone mat or a layer of parchment.

3. Whisk the eggs with cheese, flour, garlic powder, black pepper, and baking powder.

4. Scoop the dough and mix into ten biscuits - place them on the tray.

5. Bake until they are cooked through (12-15 min.).

6. Plate the biscuits and slather using melted butter over the top.

7. Finely chop the parsley and sprinkle it over the biscuits to serve.

Pink Drink

Time required:
10 minutes

Servings: 01

INGREDIENTS

1 strawberry tea bag

1 raspberry tea bag

1 cup boiling water

2 tablespoons erythritol

1½ cups ice water

¼ cup full-fat coconut milk

3 fresh strawberries

Pinch of xanthan gum

STEPS FOR COOKING

1. Place the tea bags in a mug and pour the boiling water over them.

2. Cover and steep for 5 minutes.

3. Add the erythritol and stir until completely dissolved.

4. Add ice water and stir.

5. In a blender, pulse the tea mixture, coconut milk, strawberries, and xanthan gum until smooth.

6. Serve chilled.

Keto-Friendly Buttermilk Pancakes

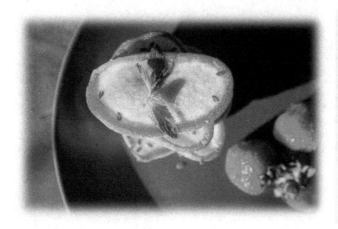

Time required:
15 minutes

Servings: 12

INGREDIENTS

2 cups of non-sifted flour

2 teaspoons of baking powder

1 teaspoon of salt

3 tablespoons of sugar

2 eggs

2 ⅓ cups of low-fat buttermilk

Butter for cooking

STEPS FOR COOKING

1. Preheat a baking sheet or large skillet to 350 ° F.

2. Place a buttered piece close to the pan; you can make it butter before preparing any pancake.

3. Beat the eggs and buttermilk in a medium bowl until well blended. Beat in the flour, baking soda, sugar, and salt. Beat thoroughly until well blended.

4. Prepare the skillet by rubbing the butter in a circle in the center, then adding about ½ cup of batter. Divide the batter until it forms an even circle.

5. When the pancake surface becomes fizzy, turn over and cook on the other side until you can't see any wet spots on the edges.

INGREDIENTS	STEPS FOR COOKING

6. Repeat with the remaining batter, making sure to sprinkle the skillet before starting each pancake. Serve with your favorite syrup or fruit.

Griddle Sandwich

Time required:
30 minutes

Servings: 06

INGREDIENTS

The Buns:

.5 cup pancake
syrup - sugar-free

Unflavored gelatin
(1 envelope/approx.
3 tsp. - Only for
Method two)

3 large eggs

3 oz. cream cheese

1 cup almond flour

2 tsp. baking
powder

1.5 tsp. vanilla
extract

1 tsp. pure maple
extract

.5 tsp. liquid stevia

The Filling:

STEPS FOR COOKING

Technique Used:

1. Cover a baking tray with a layer of
    parchment baking paper.

Method One:

1. Use a saucepan to warm the syrup
    until it's boiling using the med-high
    temperature setting, continuously
    stirring until the syrup has thickened
    and reduced by half (2-3 min.).

2. Empty the syrup onto the baking tray,
    then pop it in the freezer for 1 hour.

Method Two:

1. Use a medium temperature setting to
    make the syrup using a small
    saucepan. Transfer it to the
    countertop and whisk in gelatin
    powder till the lumps are gone.

2. Line a small dish with aluminum foil.
    Pour the syrup mixture into the dish

INGREDIENTS	STEPS FOR COOKING

INGREDIENTS

6 large eggs

Black pepper and salt, as desired

6 cheese slices

6 portions cooked sausage/sliced bacon

STEPS FOR COOKING

and pop it in the freezer while preparing the pancake batter.

3. Warm the oven to reach 350° Fahrenheit/177° Celsius.

4. Cover a baking tray with foil, then place 12 mason jar rings onto the pan. Spray the inside of the rings using a spritz of cooking oil spray.

5. Measure and add the remainder of the buns' fixings into a blender- pulse till they're smooth. Pour the batter into the rings (2-3 tbsp. each).

6. Remove the syrup from the freezer, gently remove the parchment/foil away from the syrup, cut it into small pieces, and scatter them into the batter.

7. Bake until set (12-15 min.).

8. Cool slightly before removing the sandwich from the rings.

9. For the Eggs: Prepare the eggs to your liking - scrambled or fried. Whisk the eggs with pepper and salt. Pour them into a greased 9×13 or similar baking dish.

10. Set a timer to bake till the eggs are set (15 min.). Cool, then slice them into six even portions.

11. Assemble the sandwiches using one pancake bun with one slice of bacon/sausage, one egg, and a cheese slice, and top with a second bun. Yummy!

Pumpkin Spice Frappuccino

Time required:
10 minutes

Servings: 02

INGREDIENTS

⅔ cup canned pure pumpkin

4 teaspoons instant coffee granules

1 tablespoon erythritol

1 teaspoon vanilla extract

1½ teaspoon pumpkin pie spice plus extra for sprinkling

⅔ cup unsweetened coconut milk

⅔ cup unsweetened almond milk

2 cups ice cubes

2 tablespoons whipped cream

STEPS FOR COOKING

1. Add all of the ingredients except for the whipped cream to a high-power blender and pulse until smooth.
2. Pour into two serving glasses, then top with whipped cream.
3. Sprinkle with extra pumpkin pie spice.

Sausage and Egg Muffin Breakfast Sandwich

Time required:
15 minutes

Servings: 01

INGREDIENTS

2 large eggs

1 tbsp butter

1 tbsp. mayonnaise

2 cooked sausage patties

2 slices cheese - sharp cheddar

Avocado slices

STEPS FOR COOKING

1. Prepare a big skillet using a medium-temperature setting to melt the butter.

2. Lightly oil silicone egg molds or mason jar rings and add them to the pan.

3. Break each of the eggs into the rings and use a fork to break the yolks gently.

4. Put a top on the frying pan - cook till the eggs are prepared as desired (3-4 min.). Transfer the eggs from the rings.

5. Place one of the eggs on a plate. Add half of the mayo. Top it with one of the sausage patties, a slice of cheese, and avocado.

6. Arrange the second sausage patty over the avocado and sprinkle on the

INGREDIENTS	STEPS FOR COOKING
	rest of the cheese. Spread the rest of the mayo on the second cooked egg and top it off with cheese. Serve when ready.

Keto Cheese Broccoli

Time required:
20 minutes

Servings: 04

INGREDIENTS

2 tablespoons butter

2 tablespoons flour

1 cup whipped cream

½ cup milk

¼ teaspoon salt

¼ teaspoon black pepper

½ teaspoon paprika powder

¼ teaspoon cayenne powder

½ teaspoon garlic powder

½ teaspoon ground mustard

8 ounces crisp cheddar cheese,

STEPS FOR COOKING

1. Preheat the oven to 375 ° F and coat 6 (10-ounces or so) casseroles with cooking spray.

2. Melt the butter in a large, heavy-bottomed pan or a Dutch oven. Beat in the flour. Cook and stir until the roux turns a light golden color.

3. Gradually beat in the cream and milk until smooth. Add the spices.

4. Cook over medium heat until the sauce thickens. Stir in cheese until melted.

5. Meanwhile, steam the broccoli in a separate pan until bright green but still crispy.

6. Add the broccoli to the white sauce and stir to coat.

INGREDIENTS	STEPS FOR COOKING
shredded (plus more for topping) 6–8 cups fresh broccoli florets, rinsedr	7. Spoon the broccoli and white sauce into the prepared dishes. Top with more cheese. 8. Bake for 3-5 minutes, until the cheese, melts on top and the edges are hot and bubbly.

Queso Blanco

Time required:
25 minutes

Servings: 10

INGREDIENTS

2 tablespoons olive oil

⅓ cup white onion, finely chopped

2 tablespoons jalapeño pepper, finely minced

1 pound white American cheese, cut into large pieces

½ pound Monterey Jack cheese, cut into large pieces

½ cup half-and-half

⅓ ½ cup tomatoes, chopped

2 tablespoons fresh cilantro, chopped (divided)

STEPS FOR COOKING

1. In a medium pan, heat the oil over medium-low heat and sauté the onion and jalapeño for 2–3 minutes.
2. Add the cheeses and half-and-half and stir to combine.
3. Reduce heat to low and cook for 2–3 minutes or until the cheeses are melted.
4. Add the tomato pieces, then stir to combine.
5. Stir in half of the cilantro, then remove from heat.
6. Serve garnished with the remaining cilantro and chopped jalapeño.

INGREDIENTS	STEPS FOR COOKING
1 jalapeño pepper, chopped	

Chickpea Salad

Time required:
10 minutes

Servings: 06

INGREDIENTS

28 ounces chickpeas, drained

½ red onion, chopped fine

2 cucumbers, chopped fine

¼ cup vegetable/Olive Oil

2 lemons, juiced

1 lemon, zested

1 tbsp Tahini

3 cloves garlic, crushed

2 tbsp oregano

Sea salt and dark pepper, as needed

STEPS FOR COOKING

1. Put out from the dish and merge cucumbers with chickpeas and red notes.

2. Take a small dish and whisk together the oregano, olive/vegetable oil, garlic, tahini, lemon zest, pepper, lemon juice, and sea salt.

3. Discard the salad dressing before serving.

Chicken Nuggets

Time required:
30 minutes

Servings: 08

INGREDIENTS

2 large eggs

1 cup almond flour

1 tablespoon smoked paprika

1 tablespoon celery salt

½ teaspoon garlic powder

½ teaspoon onion powder

1 teaspoon salt

½ teaspoon pepper

1 pound boneless, skinless chicken breast fillets, cut into bite-sized pieces

STEPS FOR COOKING

1. Preheat the oven to 400°F, then line a large baking sheet with parchment paper.

2. In a shallow dish, beat the eggs.

3. In another shallow dish, mix together the flour and spices.

4. Dip the chicken pieces into the beaten eggs and then coat with the flour mixture.

5. Arrange the chicken pieces on the prepared baking sheet in a single layer, then bake for 20–22 minutes, flipping once halfway through.

6. Serve warm.

Stuffed Jalapenos

Time required:
25 minutes

Servings: 08

INGREDIENTS

26 oz./740 jalapenos, pickled in a can

8 oz./230 g unchilled cream cheese

2 tbsp. green onions

1 tbsp. pimiento peppers

.25 cup keto-friendly mayonnaise

STEPS FOR COOKING

1. Slice the green onions and mince the peppers.

2. Leave the cream cheese out of the refrigerator to soften. Once it's ready, whip it with the mayo, chives, and pimientos. Stir till it's all incorporated and smooth.

3. Fill the jalapenos with the mixture and serve.

4. Cover and store any remaining jalapenos in the fridge for later.

Keto Macaroni and Cheese

Time required:
15 minutes

Servings: 02

INGREDIENTS

*2 pounds of penne
(or other) pasta*

*¾ cup of whipped
cream*

*8 ounces of Velveeta
cheese, cubed*

*½ cup of grated
cheddar*

STEPS FOR COOKING

1. Prepare the pasta according to the directions on the package, then drain and reserve 1 cup of the liquid.

2. Meanwhile, heat the cream in a separate pan over medium heat. Add the Velveeta and cheddar and stir until melted.

3. Pour the sauce over the pasta and stir. If it is too thick, add a little pasta water. Stir well.

4. Serve hot.

Grilled Sea Bass with Tahini Sauce

Time required:
20 minutes

Servings: 06

INGREDIENTS

2 pounds sea bass

1 cup
Vegetable/olive oil
tahini, paste

1 tbsp garlic,
crushed

1 tsp. salt

⅓ cup lemon juice

1 cup of water

STEPS FOR COOKING

1. Heat a grill, skillet, or casually oiled skillet at medium temperature.

2. To heat sea bass, perfectly dry with paper (kitchen) and smear on every side with olive/vegetable oil.

3. You can also use olive/vegetable oil Sprinkle to save duration.

4. Merge tahini, garlic, salt, and lemon juice in the small dish.

5. This becomes very thick—mix water casually (about 1 cup) till it reaches desired consistency.

6. Put the sea bass on a wire rack or skillet. Do not move it for 6 min. Give opportunity to seal the sea bass with a spatula and heat for another 7 min.

7. Put sea bass on the tray and mix with tahini sauce.

8. Serve with mix extra sauce.

Baby Arugula and Grilled Chicken

Time required:
40 minutes

Servings: 04

INGREDIENTS

Marinade:

½ cup of honey

½ cup of olive oil

½ teaspoon of pepper

½ cup of balsamic vinegar

Salad:

1 teaspoon of Salt

¼ cup of dijon mustard

4 chicken breasts

1 tablespoon of olive oil

A pack of bocconcini cheese (Cut each ball in half)

3 Roma tomatoes (diced)

STEPS FOR COOKING

1. Preheat your oven to 450°F.

2. Season the potatoes with pepper and salt to taste, toss with olive oil, then put into the oven and allow to roast for 20 minutes.

3. Put all the ingredients for the marinade in a bowl and whisk until well combined.

4. Cut the chicken into large slices and put into a ziplock bag, pour the marinade all over the chicken and shake to coat, then seal and let sit for 10 minutes.

5. Set your grill to medium-high and allow it to heat for a minute or two.

6. Remove the chicken from the ziplock bag and grill for 15 minutes, flipping regularly until evenly browned.

7. Rinse the arugula, then place in a colander to drain.

INGREDIENTS	STEPS FOR COOKING
2 red onions (sliced)	8. Once the chicken is cooked, remove it from heat and allow it to cool, then cut into thin slices.
1 pack of baby arugula	
2 sweet potatoes (chopped)	9. Share the roasted potatoes and vegetables between four bowls, top with sliced chicken and cheese, then serve.
1 cup of chopped carrots	

Rib Agrodolce

Time required:
2 hours

Servings: 04

INGREDIENTS

1 bay leaf

5 pounds of baby back ribs, cut in four

1 ½ teaspoon of basil

½ teaspoon of marjoram

1 carrot, chopped

2 cloves of garlic, minced

4 teaspoons of grill seasoning

½ teaspoon of thyme

½ teaspoon of lemon zest

2 tablespoons of unsalted butter

STEPS FOR COOKING

1. Set your broiler rack on the middle tier of your oven, turn to broil, then set the temperature on high and allow it to preheat for 5-10 minutes.

2. While the broiler preheats, season the ribs with the grill seasoning and allow them to stand at room temperature.

3. Lightly grease a broiler pan, then place the ribs on it and sear on both sides for 4-5 minutes.

4. Set the oven to bake and put the temperature to 300°F.

5. Put the butter in a large pan and melt over medium heat, then add onion, carrot, lemon zest, garlic, and celery. Stir and cook for 4- 5 minutes, stirring occasionally until the veggies are soft

INGREDIENTS

2 cups of low-sodium chicken broth

1 cup of diced tomatoes in juice

1 onion, chopped

2 cups of red wine

½ teaspoon of rosemary

2 tablespoons of finely chopped fresh parsley

1 rib of celery, chopped

Sauce:

¼ cup of sugar

⅓ cup + 1 tablespoon of balsamic vinegar

1 scallion, thinly sliced

Freshly ground black pepper to taste

Salt to taste

STEPS FOR COOKING

6. Add canned tomatoes with juice, wine, and broth, then stir to combine. Put in the spices, then allow to boil over high heat for 2-3 minutes.

7. Transfer the ribs to a roasting pan, top with sauce, cover with aluminum foil and bake for 60-75 minutes or until the ribs are tender.

8. Remove the ribs from the pan, then set them aside to cool.

9. To make the sauce, remove the bay leaf, then put the vegetables and liquid from the pan into a blender and process until smooth and thick (do so in batches if necessary).

10. Pour the mixture back into the pan, add sugar and vinegar, stir and bring to a boil over medium heat.

11. Allow the sauce to cook for 15-20 minutes or until the mixture reduces by half.

12. Put the rib backs on a broiler pan, drizzle some sauce over them and broil on high until browned.

13. Remove and serve garnished with scallions.

Fried Mozzarella

Time required:
20 minutes

Servings: 04

INGREDIENTS

⅔ cup almond flour

⅓ cup arrowroot starch

2 eggs, beaten

¼ cup water

1½ cups pork rinds, finely crushed

1 teaspoon Italian seasoning

½ teaspoons garlic salt

1 pound mozzarella cheese, cut into thick slices

1–2 cups olive oil

STEPS FOR COOKING

1. In a shallow bowl, mix together the flour and arrowroot starch.

2. In a second shallow bowl, lightly beat the eggs and water.

3. In a third shallow bowl, mix together the pork rinds, Italian seasoning, and garlic salt.

4. Coat the mozzarella slices with the flour mixture, then dip them into the egg mixture, and finally coat them with the pork rind mixture.

5. In a deep skillet, heat the oil over medium heat and fry the mozzarella slices in 3 batches for about 1 minute per side, then with a slotted spoon, transfer the mozzarella sticks onto a paper-towel-lined plate to drain.

Coleslaw

Time required:
10 minutes

Servings: 08

INGREDIENTS

¾ cup vegan
mayonnaise

¼ cup unsweetened
almond milk

3 tablespoons white
vinegar

1 tablespoon lemon
juice

¼ cup erythritol

1 tablespoon onion
powder

Salt and ground
white pepper, as
required

1 head green
cabbage, chopped

1 carrot, peeled and
chopped

STEPS FOR COOKING

1. In a bowl, mix the mayonnaise,
   almond milk, vinegar, lemon juice,
   erythritol, onion powder, salt, and
   white pepper until well combined.

2. In a salad bowl, mix the cabbage and
   carrot.

3. Add the dressing and toss to coat well,
   then cover and refrigerate for at least
   2–3 hours before serving.

Keto Olive Garden Salad and Creamy Dressing

Time required:
40 minutes

Servings: 04

INGREDIENTS

1 pack of Good
Seasonings Italian
Dressing

½ teaspoon of dried
Italian herbs

½ teaspoon of table
salt

¼ tsp black pepper

½ tsp sugar

¼ tsp garlic powder

½ tbsp mayonnaise

¼ cup of olive oil

2 tbsp white vinegar

1 ½ tbsp water

STEPS FOR COOKING

1. Prepare Good Seasonings Italian
   Seasonings Dressing as it says on the
   back of the package (mix with oil,
   water, and vinegar in the dimensions
   on the package)

2. Once prepared to pour into a medium
   bowl, add any additional substances
   indexed above (starting with dried
   Italian herbs).

3. Mix all the elements with a whisk until
   well blended.

4. Serve with your favorite salads.

Chicken Bryan

Time required:
50 minutes

Servings: 04

INGREDIENTS

¾ cup dry white wine

4 boneless, skinless chicken breasts

8 tablespoons of butter

2 tablespoons of chopped basil

8 ounces of goat cheese

½ teaspoon of salt

2 tablespoons of sun-dried tomatoes

2 tablespoons of lemon juice

¼ teaspoon of freshly ground black pepper

STEPS FOR COOKING

To Make Chicken:

1. Place the chicken between two pieces of plastic wrap and pound until half an inch thick, then remove, rinse and pat dry with a paper towel.

2. Season the chicken with pepper and salt, then brush with olive oil until properly coated.

3. Grill chicken for 3-4 minutes on each side or until golden brown, then remove and plate before covering with plastic wrap to keep warm.

4. Slice the goat cheese into four for each piece of chicken and set aside until ready to use.

To Make Sauce:

1. Sauté the garlic and onions in two tablespoons of butter over medium heat until fragrant, about 3-4 minutes.

INGREDIENTS

*2 tablespoons of
olive oil*

*2 teaspoons of
chopped garlic*

*¼ cup of chopped
white onions*

STEPS FOR COOKING

2. Add lemon juice and wine, then allow to simmer until the mixture loses half its moisture, then add three tablespoons of butter and stir until fully melted and well incorporated.

3. Turn off the heat and add the rest of the butter and stir until melted and sauce is thick.

4. Strain the sauce to remove garlic and onion, then pour back into the pan and add the tomatoes and basil.

5. Put the chicken on a serving platter, place the mozzarella slices on each piece of chicken then drizzle a generous amount of sauce over it.

6. Serve and enjoy!

Egg Drop Soup

Time required:
20 minutes

Servings: 06

INGREDIENTS

1 egg

2 teaspoons toasted sesame oil, divided

1 ½ quarts chicken broth

Salt as required

¼ teaspoon ground white pepper

3 scallion greens, sliced

STEPS FOR COOKING

1. In a small bowl, slightly beat the egg with 1 teaspoon of sesame oil. Set aside.

2. Add the broth to a pan and bring to a boil over medium-low heat.

3. Slowly stir in the egg mixture.

4. Stir in the remaining sesame oil, salt, and white pepper.

5. Simmer for 4–5 minutes or until soup reaches desired thickness, stirring continuously.

6. Serve hot garnished with scallions.

Cheese Chicken Penne

Time required:
45 minutes

Servings: 02

INGREDIENTS

.33 cup Italian Salad Seasoning

2 chicken breasts

15 oz. Alfredo sauce

4 tomatoes

2-3 cloves garlic

1 tsp. basil

3 cups penne pasta

8 oz. Italian cheese, shredded/parmesan /mozzarella, or provolone

6 tbsp. olive oil

STEPS FOR COOKING

1. Chop the chicken breasts. After chopping them, marinate the chicken pieces in the Italian dressing for thirty minutes.

2. Make the bruschetta. Chop the tomatoes and mince the garlic into a mixing container. Mix in the basil and toss, setting it aside for now.

3. In a pot of water, cook the penne.

4. Cook the chicken using the broiling or grilling method.

5. Take two microwave-safe bowls to toss the cooked pasta - divide it equally between the two bowls.

6. Over the pasta, pour the alfredo sauce. Repeat the procedure for the second microwavable bowl.

7. On it, add the chicken. It should form a layer over the pasta and sauce.

8. Microwave for three minutes. If you are using the previous chilled chicken, microwave till the cheese melts.

9. Serve the delicious dish with garlic bread.

Keto Hot N 'Spicy Buffalo Wings

Time required:
15 minutes

Servings: 02

INGREDIENTS

*5 pounds of chicken
wings, cut into half*

*2 cups of whole
wheat flour*

*1 cup all-purpose
flour*

*2 1/2 teaspoons of
salt*

*1 teaspoon of
paprika*

*1/4 teaspoon of
cayenne pepper*

STEPS FOR COOKING

1. In a large mixing bowl, combine flour, salt, paprika, and cayenne pepper and mix well. Cut chicken wings into drumettes and flappers. Wash the poultry and let it drain. Cover the bird with flour aggregate; put bird wings in the fridge for 90 minutes.

2. Spread the chicken in the flour mixture; Put chicken wings in the refrigerator for 90 minutes.

3. If equipped to fry chicken wings, heat the oil to reach 375. Place the poultry pieces in heated oil, but do not compress them. Fry the chicken wings until golden brown. Remove from oil and drain.

4. When all the wings are cooked, place them in a huge bowl. Add Hot Sauce aggregate and mix well.

5. Use a fork to place chicken pieces on a serving platter, then serve now and with plenty of kitchen paper.

Pesto Pasta

Time required:
35 minutes

Servings: 01

INGREDIENTS

*13 oz. whole wheat
pasta*
1 garlic clove
1 bunch of basil
*1 cup of
olive/vegetable oil*
2 oz. of pine nuts
Salt Parmesan

STEPS FOR COOKING

1. In a mixer, merge the basil, garlic, some Parmesan cheese, butter, pine nuts, and some salt.
2. Heat the pasta in the salted boiling water and remove water.
3. Put the pesto over the pasta and heat for 1 min.

Chicken Alfredo Pizza

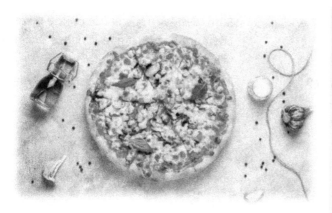

Time required:
40 minutes

Servings: 04

INGREDIENTS

¼ cup of flour

1 (12-inch size) store-bought pizza dough

¼ cup sliced green onions

¼ teaspoon of pepper

2 tablespoons of grated Parmesan cheese

2 teaspoons of olive oil

¼ cup of shredded Asiago cheese

2 boneless, skinless chicken breasts, sliced

STEPS FOR COOKING

1. Preheat your oven to 425°F.

2. Grease a 12-inch pizza pan and spread the dough out until it is barely touching the edges of the pan.

3. Put into the oven and allow to bake for 5-7 minutes or until the crust is golden.

4. Put the flour, salt, and pepper into a zip-lock bag, seal and shake to combine, then add the chicken and toss to coat.

5. Remove the chicken and pat off the excess flour before placing it on a piece of waxed paper.

6. Put the oil into a large skillet and cook the chicken over medium heat until the crust is brown and crispy.

7. Remove from the heat, then put in a colander to drain.

INGREDIENTS

¾ cup of Alfredo sauce

½ teaspoon of salt

½ cup of shredded mozzarella cheese

3 cloves of garlic, minced

STEPS FOR COOKING

8. Spread the Alfredo sauce on the pizza crust until it is just a few inches shy of touching the edge.

9. Top with the fried chicken, then sprinkle with Asiago, Parmesan, mozzarella, and green onions.

10. Put the pizza back into the oven and bake for 10 more minutes or until the cheese is melted at the top.

Chicken Limone

Time required:
40 minutes

Servings: 04

INGREDIENTS

1 egg

3 tablespoons lemon juice, divided

⅓ cup almond flour

⅛ teaspoon paprika

⅛ teaspoon garlic powder

4 boneless, skinless chicken breasts, pounded

¼ cup butter

2 teaspoons chicken bouillon

½ cup hot water

1 tablespoon capers

STEPS FOR COOKING

1. In a shallow bowl, beat the egg with 1 tablespoon of lemon juice.

2. In another shallow bowl, mix the flour, paprika, and garlic powder.

3. Dip each chicken breast in the egg mixture and then coat it with the flour mixture.

4. In a large skillet, melt the butter over medium-high heat and cook the chicken breasts for 2–3 minutes per side.

5. Meanwhile, in a small bowl, dissolve the bouillon in the hot water.

6. Stir in the bouillon mixture and remaining lemon juice into the skillet and bring to a boil.

7. Reduce heat to low and simmer for 10–15 minutes.

8. Serve hot garnished with capers.

Bacon-Wrapped Tuna

Time required:
20 minutes

Servings: 02

INGREDIENTS

4 tbsp. honey

Salt and pepper

.25 cup
Worcestershire
sauce

.5 cup soy sauce

4 slices bacon

16 oz. tuna fillets

STEPS FOR COOKING

1. Wrap small portions of tuna with the bacon slices. Secure them by folding them with the help of toothpicks. Put them on the grill.

2. Combine the honey with the soy sauce and Worcestershire sauce - brush the mixture over the wrapped tunas.

3. Cook them until they are thoroughly cooked - till the tuna's color starts to lighten, and the bacon starts sizzling.

4. Flip them over. Cook until done. (Preferably medium-rare to medium).

5. Again brush the tuna with the sauce. Season with black pepper, and then serve.

Chicken Enchilada Soup

Time required:
28 minutes

Servings: 03

INGREDIENTS

2 rotisserie chickens or 3 pounds of cooked, diced chicken

½ pound of processed American cheese; cut into small cubes

3 cups yellow onions, diced

¼ cup chicken crust

2 cups Masa Harina

½ teaspoon cayenne pepper

2 teaspoons garlic granules

1 or 2 teaspoons salt

STEPS FOR COOKING

1. In a large saucepan over medium heat, combine the oil with onions, chicken base, garlic granules, chili powder, cumin, cayenne, and salt. Cook for 3 to 5 minutes until the onions are soft and translucent, stirring occasionally.

2. Mix 1 liter of water with masa Harina in a large cup or jug.

3. Keep stirring until there are no more lumps. Add the onions; Bring the mixture to a boil over medium heat.

4. Once ready, cook for a few minutes. Stir in tomatoes and the remaining 3 liters of water. Bring the soup to a boil again, stirring occasionally. Add the cheese.

5. Cook until cheese is completely melted, stirring occasionally. Add the

INGREDIENTS

2 cups tomatoes, crushed

½ cup vegetable oil

2 teaspoons chili powder

4 liters water

2 teaspoons ground cumin

STEPS FOR COOKING

chicken and cook until well heated. Serve immediately and enjoy.

Panda Express Mandarin Chicken

Time required:
25 minutes

Servings: 04

INGREDIENTS

2/3 cup sugar

¼ cup soy sauce

1 tbsp lemon juice

1 tsp. vegetable oil

1 tsp. fresh garlic, crushed

½ tsp. fresh ginger, crushed

4 tbsp arrowroot

¼ cup water

6 skinless chicken thighs

STEPS FOR COOKING

1. Heat the grill to high heat.

2. In the small frypan, merge the lemon juice, soy sauce, sugar, ginger, garlic, and oil.

3. In a separate small dish, merge a pinch of water and mix well. arrow allowed. Mix the apricot blend to the skillet and heat at high temperature.

4. Mixrepeatedlytill the blend boils, decrease heat and boil 4-6 pieces. min or till the sauce thickens.

5. Rub every piece of chicken with the oil when the grill is hot and sauté 4 to 6 min on every side or till fully cooked. The chicken must have gold spots.

6. When the chicken is cooked, cut it into small pieces. We throw the pieces in the big fry pan at medium

INGREDIENTS	STEPS FOR COOKING
	temperature. Heat till chicken is sifted, decrease heat, and seal till tender be present.
	7. Put the chicken in the medium dish and mix with the sauce on the chicken's top and mix till sealed well.

Olive Tapenade

Time required:
15 minutes

Servings: 07

INGREDIENTS

½ teaspoon of thyme

1 ½ cups of pitted green olives

1 loaf of Italian bread

¼ cup of capers

1 cup of extra virgin olive oil

2 ½ cups of pitted black olives

½ teaspoon of salt

½ teaspoon of dried crushed oregano

1 tablespoon of minced garlic

STEPS FOR COOKING

1. Put the capers, black olives, olive oil, garlic, green olives, pepper, oregano, salt, thyme, and lemon juice into a food processor and pulse until smooth.

2. Transfer the mixture to a container, cover, and refrigerate until ready to use.

3. Combine 1 teaspoon of minced garlic and 4 tablespoons of extra-virgin olive oil in a small bowl, then slice the bread into four.

4. Brush the bread slices with olive oil mixture on both sides of the Italian bread.

5. Grill both sides of the bread until golden brown. Remove from heat, then cut each piece in half.

INGREDIENTS

½ teaspoon of freshly ground black pepper

2 tablespoons of fresh lemon juice

STEPS FOR COOKING

6. Put the olive tapenade in a small bowl and serve with grilled Italian bread on the side.

Instant Pot General Tso Chicken

Time required:
27 minutes

Servings: 04

INGREDIENTS

Sauce:

3 cloves garlic, minced

½ teaspoon fresh ginger, minced

5 tablespoons low-sodium soy sauce

2 tablespoons sugar-free ketchup

1 teaspoon sesame oil

1 teaspoon chili paste

1 teaspoon erythritol

Chicken:

STEPS FOR COOKING

1. In a bowl, beat all of the sauce ingredients until well combined.

2. Season the chicken pieces with salt and pepper, then place the almond flour in a shallow dish.

3. Dip the chicken pieces in the egg and then coat them with the flour.

4. Place the oil in the Instant Pot, then select SAUTE. Add the chicken pieces, then cook for 3–4 minutes.

5. Add the broth and scrape the brown bits from the bottom, then select CANCEL and stir in the sauce.

6. Secure the lid and place the pressure valve in the SEAL position.

7. Select MANUAL and cook under high pressure for about 4 minutes.

INGREDIENTS

1½ pounds boneless chicken thighs, cut into little pieces

¼ teaspoon salt

¼ teaspoon pepper

2 egg whites, beaten

½ cup almond flour

2 tablespoons coconut oil

½ cup chicken broth

½ teaspoon xanthan gum

STEPS FOR COOKING

8. Select CANCEL and carefully do a quick pressure release.

9. Remove the lid and select SAUTE.

10. Immediately stir in the xanthan gum and cook for 1–2 minutes or until the sauce thickens.

11. Select CANCEL and serve hot.

Country Fried Flounder

Time required:
30 minutes

Servings: 06

INGREDIENTS

Oil, as needed

.5 tsp. each paprika

.5 tsp. each salt and black pepper

1 cup cornmeal

2 lb./910 g flounder fillets

STEPS FOR COOKING

1. Skin the pieces of fish, and cut them into medium-sized slices.

2. Take a container and add the cornmeal, black pepper, paprika, and salt.

3. Turn on the oven. Pour oil into a skillet to warm using a med-high temperature setting.

4. Rub the fillets in the cornmeal mixture and put them into the pan of oil.

5. Cook the fillets for about two to three minutes until their color turns golden brown. Turn the fillet to the opposite side and cook for another two to three minutes. Check whether it is properly cooked or not with the help of a fork. If it flakes easily, then it is perfectly cooked.

INGREDIENTS	STEPS FOR COOKING
	6. Take the fish from the pan, put it over a paper towel, and drain it. Serve it hot.

Classic Cheesecake

Time required:
15 minutes

Servings: 02

INGREDIENTS

Crust:

1½ cups of Graham
Cracker Crumbs

¼ teaspoon of
cinnamon, ground

⅓ cup of margarine,
melted

Filling:

4-8 ounce packages
of cream cheese
softened

1 ¼ cup of white
sugar

½ cup of sour cream

2 teaspoons vanilla
extract

5 large eggs

Topping:

STEPS FOR COOKING

1. Preheat the oven to 475 ° F and heat a large skillet with ½ inch of water in it.

2. Combine crust ingredients in a bowl. A large cake tin lined with baking paper spread the crust on the pan and press firmly. Cover with foil and keep in the freezer until use.

3. Mix the ingredients for the filling, except for eggs, in a bowl, then whisk the bowl until the mixture is smooth.

4. Stir in the eggs and beat until completely mixed.

5. Remove the crust from the freezer and add the filling to the crust, distributing evenly. Place the pie pan in a heated water bath (skillet in the oven) and bake for about 12 minutes. Reduce heat to 350 °F. Continue to cook for about 50 minutes or until the

INGREDIENTS

½ cup of sour cream

2 teaspoons of sugar

STEPS FOR COOKING

top is golden brown. Remove from oven and place skillet on a wire rack to cool.

6. For the topping, mix all the ingredients in a bowl. Brush the cake with the topping and cover. Keep in the refrigerator for at least 4 hours.

7. Serve cold.

Zabaglione

Time required:
30 minutes

Servings: 02

INGREDIENTS

½ cup fresh strawberries, hulled and sliced

3 tablespoons + 1 teaspoon erythritol, divided

¼ cup dry Marsala wine

3 large egg yolks

STEPS FOR COOKING

1. In a bowl, gently toss the strawberries with 1 teaspoon of erythritol to coat.

2. Cover and set aside at room temperature for about 1 hour.

3. Divide the strawberries into 2 small serving bowls.

4. In a small pan, add the wine, egg yolk, and remaining erythritol over low heat and cook for 7–8 minutes, beating continuously.

5. Remove from heat and pour the custard over the strawberries.

6. Serve warm.

Frosty Chocolate Shake

Time required:
10 minutes

Servings: 02

INGREDIENTS

1 cup heavy whipping cream

1 tbsp. almond butter

2 tbsp. unsweetened cocoa powder

.5 tsp. liquid stevia sweetener

1 tsp. vanilla extract

STEPS FOR COOKING

1. Combine each of the fixings and combine using an electric mixer till you create stiff peaks.

2. Pop the container into the freezer for 30 minutes to an hour till it's barely frozen.

3. Scoop it into a plastic bag, cut out a corner, and squeeze to serve it into a couple of cute cups.

Chocolate Bread Pudding

Time required:
20 minutes

Servings: 02

INGREDIENTS

For the Bread Pudding:

5 cups of challah or challah bread

1 cup of whole milk

1 cup of heavy cream

¾ cups of chocolate chips

½ cup of sugar

¼ cup of bitter cocoa powder

2 eggs

1 tablespoon of unsalted butter

1 teaspoon of cinnamon powder

½ teaspoon of salt

STEPS FOR COOKING

1. Cut the bread into small cubes. While you can use fresh food as is, hard bread will absorb drinks much better. If you are using fresh bread, lightly toast the cubes by spreading them out on a baking tray and placing them in the 180 ° C oven for 10 minutes.

2. Combine bitter powder, sugar, salt, floor cinnamon, heavy cream, whole milk, vanilla extract, and eggs in a large bowl.

3. Add the baked pieces and chips and let the mixture sit for an hour to allow the bread to absorb the liquid.

4. Preheat oven to 180 ° C. Spread a 10 x 7-inch baking dish with butter and pour in the bread and liquid aggregate.

INGREDIENTS

1 teaspoon of vanilla extract

For Cover:

¼ cup of chocolate chips

¼ cup of heavy cream

STEPS FOR COOKING

5. Place the pan on a baking sheet and bake for 40 minutes or until the mixture is set.

6. Cover by melting the chocolate chips in the microwave for several seconds and stirring the cream until smooth. Pour the topping over the chocolate bread pudding and serve warm or at room temperature.

Keto Mint Chocolate Brownies

Time required:
25 minutes

Servings: 02

INGREDIENTS

For the Brownie:

180 g dark chocolate

1¼ cup of sugar

100 g unsalted butter

2/3 cup 0000 flour

3 eggs

1 tablespoon of bitter cocoa powder

½ teaspoon of vanilla extract

½ teaspoon of salt

For the Buttercream with Mint:

100 g unsalted butter

90 g cream cheese

STEPS FOR COOKING

1. Preheat the oven to 180 ° C.

2. Melt the butter and finely chopped dark chocolate in a water bath or microwave, and place aggregate in a large bowl.

3. Add the sugar and mix with a cord beater and add the salt, vanilla extract, sour cocoa powder, and eggs.

4. Finally, add the flour and process with enveloping movements. Thoroughly mix until you get a homogeneous mixture.

5. Pour the brownie instruction onto an 8 "x 11" that was previously protected with molding paper and bake for 25 minutes or until it comes out dry while inserting a toothpick. Let cool on a rack. Put the butter in small cubes in a

INGREDIENTS

2½ cups of
powdered sugar

5 drops of green
food coloring

1 pinch of salt

1½ teaspoons of
mint extract

For Cover:

240 g dark chocolate

5 tablespoons of
unsalted butter

STEPS FOR COOKING

blender and mix with the cream cheese until you get a creamy result.

6. Add the mint and then the inexperienced edible coloring. Finally, upload the powdered sugar a little at a time. Beat on low speed until a homogeneous aggregate is obtained.

7. Divide the mint buttercream over the bloodless brownie and cover it with paper, then keep in the fridge for 30 minutes.

8. Melt the chocolate and butter in a water bath or the microwave and pour the mint cream on top. Spread with a spatula and put back in the refrigerator for an additional 30 minutes.

Chocolate Mousse Cake

Time required:
35 minutes

Servings: 06

INGREDIENTS

1 (18.25 ounce) cake mix pack-chocolate

1 can (14 ounces) condensed milk-sweeten

2 dices (1 ounce) unsweetened chocolate, liquefied

½ cup cold water

1 package (3.9 ounces) instant pudding mix chocolate

1 cup whipped heavy cream

STEPS FOR COOKING

1. Turn on the heat of the microwave at around 175 degrees Celsius.

2. Keep Heating and bake the cookies in the two layers (9 inches) following the package directions.

3. Cool and the bread translucent. Mergeliquefied chocolate milk and then condensed in the big box bath. Mix the water calmly and mix the pudding instantly till it softens.

4. Freeze for 30 minminimum. Put out the chocolate blend from the freezer and beat till soft.

5. Written by Whip the cream and freeze for a minimum of an hour. Put one of the baking trays on a tray.

6. Includes 1 1/2 mousse cups and seal with the rest of the crust. Frost with

INGREDIENTS	STEPS FOR COOKING
	the rest of the mousse, and let cool till served.
	7. Decorate with chocolate or fresh fruit.

Vera's Lemon Cookies

Time required:
30 minutes

Servings: 04

INGREDIENTS

1 cup of
confectioners' sugar

¾ cup of softened
unsalted butter

1 teaspoon of lemon
zest (grated lemon
zest before juicing)

2 egg yolks

2 tablespoons of
freshly squeezed
lemon juice

½ teaspoon of
vanilla extract

2 cups of all-purpose
flour

¼ teaspoon of
kosher salt

STEPS FOR COOKING

1. Combine the sugar and butter in a
   bowl and mix until fluffy using an
   electric mixer.

2. Add vanilla, egg yolks, and salt, mix
   again until well combined.

3. Add the flour, small amounts at a time
   until well incorporated.

4. Cut the dough in half, then roll each
   piece into one-inch logs.

5. Wrap the logs in wax paper and
   refrigerate for 25-30 minutes or until
   firm.

6. Preheat your oven to 350°F.

7. Cut the logs into slightly thick, round
   pieces and place them on a
   parchment-lined baking sheet,
   keeping them at least an inch apart.

INGREDIENTS	STEPS FOR COOKING
¾ cup of granulated sugar	8. Bake for 15-20 minutes or until golden.
	9. Remove from the oven and let cool on the baking sheet for 5-10 minutes, then move the cookies to a cooling rack.
	10. Combine the lemon juice, confectioners' sugar, and lemon zest in a small bowl and whisk until thick, then dip each cookie in the glaze and let sit for 15 minutes or until the glaze sets completely.

Glazed Doughnuts

Time required:
30 minutes

Servings: 06

INGREDIENTS

Doughnuts:

2 eggs

½ cup almond flour

¼ cup unsweetened protein powder

2 tablespoons coconut flour

¼ cup erythritol

¼ teaspoon salt

2 teaspoons baking powder

1 teaspoon vanilla extract

⅛–¼ cup unsweetened vanilla almond milk

Glaze:

¼ cup butter, melted

STEPS FOR COOKING

1. Preheat the oven to 350°F.
2. Grease a doughnut pan.
3. In a bowl, mix together all of the doughnut ingredients.
4. Fill each prepared doughnut hole about ¾ full with the mixture.
5. Bake for about 14–16 minutes or until the top becomes golden brown.
6. Remove from the oven, then place the pan on a wire rack to cool completely.
7. In a bowl, beat all of the glaze ingredients until well combined.
8. Spread the glaze over the doughnuts and serve.

INGREDIENTS

¼ cup erythritol
1 teaspoon vanilla
extract

STEPS FOR COOKING

Cold Lemon Dices

Time required:
30 minutes

Servings: 04

INGREDIENTS

*1 cup avocado oil +
a drizzle*

*2 bananas, peeled
and cut*

1 Tbsp honey

¼ cup lemon juice

*A pinch of lemon
zest, peeved*

STEPS FOR COOKING

1. In a food processor, merge bananas with other components, press well, and put them on the bottom of the skillet, oiled with few drops of oil.

2. Freeze for 30 min, cut into cubes and serve.

Tiramisu

Time required:
15 minutes

Servings: 02

INGREDIENTS

Base:

¼ cup almond flour

1-3 teaspoons powdered erythritol

Pinch of ground cinnamon

Pinch of salt

1½ teaspoons unsalted butter melted

1 teaspoon strong brewed coffee

Tiramisu:

2 ½ tablespoons heavy cream

⅓ cup mascarpone cheese softened

STEPS FOR COOKING

1. For the base: heat a dry skillet over medium heat and toast the almond flour for 2–4 minutes or until golden and fragrant, stirring continuously.

2. Remove from heat, then transfer to a small bowl.

3. Add the erythritol, cinnamon, and salt and mix well.

4. Add the butter and coffee and mix well.

5. For the tiramisu: In a bowl, beat the heavy cream with an electric mixer until whipped.

6. Add the mascarpone cheese, erythritol, and wine and mix well.

7. Divide the base mixture into two serving glasses.

INGREDIENTS

2–3 tablespoons powdered erythritol

1 tablespoon dry white wine

Cocoa powder, for dusting

STEPS FOR COOKING

8. Top with the cream mixture, then refrigerate for 2 hours or up to overnight.

9. Dust with cocoa powder and serve.

York Peppermint Patties

Time required:
20 minutes

Servings: 07

INGREDIENTS

4 cups of powdered sugar

1/3 cup of corn syrup

1/3 cup of butter

4 or 5 drops of peppermint extract

8 grams of dark chocolate

1 tablespoon of vegetable fat

STEPS FOR COOKING

1. Strain the confectioners' sugar.

2. Add sugar, corn syrup, butter, and peppermint extract to a medium bowl. Blend until clean with a mixer.

3. The mint candy is served in bite-sized balls. Excellent for about 20 minutes. Press the patties with the bottom of a glass when you're ready for dipping.

4. Melt the chocolate in a double boiler and briefly reduce.

5. Drop the melted chocolate into the peppermint patties, flip them over and place the dipped peppermint patties on both a Silpat mat and wax paper to dry.

Keto Chocolate Flan

Time required:
16 minutes

Servings: 03

INGREDIENTS

For the Candy:
100 g of sugar
For the Chocolate
Pie:
8 eggs
700 ml of milk
200 g dark chocolate
1 tablespoon of
sugar

STEPS FOR COOKING

1. Put the sugar in a pan or in the tin to place the flan and make the caramel.

2. Peel the eggs and put them in a bowl. Beat them loose with a few string rods.

3. Mix the eggs with the milk, a spoonful of sugar, and the chopped and melted chocolate in the microwave or a water bath. Integrate with the sticks and pour the homemade chocolate pie practice into the pie over the caramel.

4. Place the mold in a container with water. Bring to the oven and cook dinner in a 180 ° C water bath for 40 minutes.

CPSIA information can be obtained
at www.ICGtesting.com
Printed in the USA
BVHW091403250521
608095BV00002B/294